D1370749

101 BREAKFAST & BRUNCH *Recipes*

Grandma's Warm Breakfast Fruit, page 61

Pennsylvania Dutch Scrapple, page 73

Bacon & Egg Potato Skins, page 41

Gooseberry Patch
2500 Farmers Dr., #110
Columbus, OH 43235

www.gooseberrypatch.com
1•800•854•6673

Copyright 2012, Gooseberry Patch 978-1-61281-085-0
First Printing, May, 2012

Gooseberry Patch *cookbooks*

Since 1992, we've been publishing our own country cookbooks for every kitchen and for every meal of the day! Each title has hundreds of budget-friendly recipes, using ingredients you already have on hand in your pantry.

In addition, you'll find helpful tips and ideas on every page, along with our hand-drawn artwork and plenty of personality. Their lay-flat binding makes them so easy to use...they're sure to become a fast favorite in your kitchen.

Texas Toads in the Hole, page 39

Orange-Cinnamon French Toast, page 49

Call us toll-free at
1•800•854•6673
and we'd be delighted to tell you all about our newest titles!

Shop with us online anytime at
www.gooseberrypatch.com

Send us your favorite recipe!

and the memory that makes it special for you!* If we select your recipe for a brand-new **Gooseberry Patch** cookbook, your name will appear right along with it...and you'll receive a FREE copy of the book!

Submit your recipe on our website at
www.gooseberrypatch.com

Or mail to:

Gooseberry Patch • Attn: Cookbook Dept.
2500 Farmers Dr., #110 • Columbus, OH 43235

*Please include the number of servings and all other necessary information!

Have a taste for more?

Visit www.gooseberrypatch.com
to join our **Circle of Friends**!

- Free recipes, tips and ideas plus a complete cookbook index
- Get special email offers and our monthly eLetter delivered to your inbox
- Find local stores with **Gooseberry Patch** cookbooks, calendars and organizers

Cranberry-Orange Warmer, page 71

PB&J Breakfast Bars, page 27

Best-Ever Brunch Potatoes, page 63

Barbara's Open-House Waffles, page 33

Raised Doughnuts, page 96

Farmers' Market Omelet, page 47

Milk & Honey Couscous, page 11

CONTENTS

Dilled Crab Egg Cups, page 67

Dedication

To all those early-risers who love to eat a homemade breakfast while watching the sun come up.

Appreciation

A million thanks to the wonderful cooks who sent us their best and brightest breakfast & brunch recipes!

Fiesta Corn Tortilla Quiche, page 68

Break-of-Day Berry Parfait

1 c. strawberries, hulled and
    sliced
1/2 c. raspberries
1/4 c. blackberries
1 c. bran & raisin cereal
6-oz. container strawberry
    yogurt

In a bowl, combine berries; divide
into 2 small bowls. Top each with
cereal. Spoon yogurt over top.
Serves 2.

7

Michelle Case
Yardley, PA

So pretty served in a
parfait or champagne glass!

Kelly's Easy Caramel Rolls

3 T. corn syrup, divided
3 T. brown sugar, packed and
 divided
3 T. chopped pecans, divided
2 T. butter, cubed and divided
12-oz. tube refrigerated biscuits

To each of 10 greased muffin cups,
add one teaspoon each of syrup,
brown sugar and pecans. Top each
with 1/2 teaspoon butter and one
biscuit. Bake at 400 degrees for
8 to 10 minutes, until golden. Invert
rolls onto a plate before serving.
Makes 10 rolls.

Kelly Marshall
Olathe, KS

This is a much-requested
family recipe!

Frosty Orange Juice

6-oz. can frozen orange juice
  concentrate, partially thawed
1 c. milk
1 c. water
1 t. vanilla extract
1/3 c. sugar
12 ice cubes

Process all ingredients together in a
blender until frothy. Serve in tall
glasses. Makes 4 servings.

9

Tiffany Classen
Wichita, KS
Thick, frosty and
very refreshing!

Grab & Go Breakfast Cookies

1/2 c. butter, softened
1/2 c. sugar
1 egg, beaten
2 T. frozen orange juice
    concentrate, thawed
1 T. orange zest
1-1/4 c. all-purpose flour
1 t. baking powder
1/2 c. wheat & barley cereal

Blend together butter and sugar in a bowl until light and fluffy. Beat in egg, orange juice and zest; set aside. Combine flour and baking powder in a small bowl; stir into butter mixture until blended. Stir in cereal. Drop by tablespoonfuls, 2 inches apart, on an ungreased baking sheet. Bake at 350 degrees for 10 to 12 minutes, until golden around edges. Cool on a wire rack. Makes 1-1/2 dozen.

Penny Sherman
Cumming, GA

These cookies are perfect for those busy mornings when you have to rush out the door.

Milk & Honey Couscous

2 c. milk
2 T. honey
1 T. cinnamon
2 c. couscous, uncooked
1/3 c. dried apricots, chopped
1/3 c. raisins
1/2 c. slivered almonds

Combine milk, honey and cinnamon
in a saucepan over medium heat.
Bring to a boil; stir in couscous.
Remove from heat; cover and let
stand for 5 minutes. Fold in
remaining ingredients. Serves 6.

11

Melanie Lowe
Dover, DE

This quick-to-fix breakfast
is perfect for those chilly
mornings when you need
something to fill you up
and keep you warm.

Slow-Cooker Breakfast Casserole

32-oz. pkg. frozen diced potatoes
1 lb. bacon, diced and cooked
1 onion, diced
1 green pepper, diced
1/2 c. shredded Monterey Jack
  cheese
1 doz. eggs
1 c. milk
1 t. salt
1 t. pepper

Layer 1/3 each of potatoes, bacon, onion, green pepper and cheese. Repeat layers 2 more times, ending with a layer of cheese. In a bowl, beat together eggs, milk, salt and pepper. Pour over mixture in slow cooker. Cover and cook on low setting for 8 to 9 hours. Serves 8 to 10.

Felice Jones
Boise, ID

This is a perfect recipe for busy mornings. You wake up, the house smells so good and breakfast is ready as soon as you are.

Honeyed Fruit & Rice

2 c. cooked jasmine rice
1/3 c. dried cranberries
1/3 c. dried apricots, chopped
1/4 c. honey
Garnish: milk

Stir together hot cooked rice,
cranberries, apricots and honey.
Divide into 2 bowls; top with milk.
Makes 2 servings.

13

Marilyn Epley
Stillwater, OK

Jasmine rice is also known
as fragrant rice and can
be found in many markets
or specialty stores.

Cheese & Chive Scrambled Eggs

6 eggs, beaten
1/4 t. lemon pepper
1 T. fresh chives, chopped
1/8 t. garlic salt
1 T. butter
1/3 c. shredded Colby Jack cheese
1/3 c. cream cheese, softened

In a bowl, combine eggs, pepper, chives and salt; set aside. Melt butter in a skillet over medium-low heat; add egg mixture. Stir to scramble, cooking until set. Remove from heat; stir in cheeses until melted. Serves 2 to 3.

Deborah Wells
Broken Arrow, OK

Paired with crisp bacon and hot biscuits, this is one dish we love so much I've even served it for dinner!

Johnny Appleseed Toast

4 slices cinnamon-raisin bread
1-1/2 T. butter, divided
1 Gala apple, cored and sliced
4 t. honey
1 t. cinnamon

Spread each slice of bread with one teaspoon of butter. Cover each bread slice with an apple slice; drizzle with one teaspoon honey and sprinkle with cinnamon. Place topped bread slices on an ungreased baking sheet. Broil on high for one to 2 minutes, until toasted and golden. Makes 4 servings.

15

Rebekah Spooner
Huntsville, AL

I'm a teacher, and we make this every fall to celebrate Johnny Appleseed with our little ones in September.

Feel-Good Shake

2 bananas, sliced
2 c. milk
2 c. non-fat vanilla yogurt
1 c. pineapple juice
1 T. honey

Process all ingredients together in
a blender until smooth. Pour into a
tall glass. Serve immediately. Makes
one serving.

Patti Boepple
Trinidad, CO

This shake is a perfect way
to start your day. One sip
and you'll be hooked.

Butterscotch Granola

10 c. long-cooking oats,
 uncooked
2 sleeves graham crackers,
 crushed
2 c. sweetened flaked coconut
1 c. pecans, finely chopped
3/4 c. brown sugar, packed
1 t. baking soda
1 t. salt
2 c. butter, melted
16-oz. pkg. butterscotch chips

Mix together all ingredients except
butterscotch chips in a deep, greased
13"x9" baking pan or a roaster pan.
Bake at 300 degrees for 40 minutes,
stirring every 10 minutes. Add
butterscotch chips during the last
5 minutes; mix well after melted to
distribute evenly. Cool. Store in an
airtight container. Makes 5 quarts.

17

Alicia Sauvageau
East Wenatchee, WA
This is the best granola
I have ever eaten. My kids
and husband love it over
berry yogurt!

Busy-Morning Banana Bread

3 ripe bananas, mashed
3 eggs, beaten
1/2 c. butter, melted and slightly
   cooled
1 T. vanilla extract
1/2 c. water
18-1/2 oz. pkg. yellow cake mix

In a large bowl, blend together
bananas, eggs, butter, vanilla and
water. Gradually add dry cake mix.
Beat with an electric mixer on high
speed for 4 minutes. Pour batter into
2 greased 9"x5" loaf pans. Bake at
350 degrees for 40 minutes. Increase
temperature to 400 degrees and bake
an additional 5 to 10 minutes, until
tops are golden. Makes 2 loaves.

Laura Justice
Indianapolis, IN
Super easy and freezes well.
Just pull from the freezer
the night before and
it will be ready for
your busy morning!

Huevos Rancheros to Go-Go

2 c. green tomatillo salsa
4 eggs
1-1/2 c. shredded Monterey Jack
   cheese
4 8-inch corn tortillas

Lightly coat a skillet with non-stick vegetable spray and place over medium heat. Pour salsa into skillet; bring to a simmer. With a spoon, make 4 wells in salsa and crack an egg into each well, taking care not to break the yolks. Reduce heat to low; cover and poach eggs for 3 minutes. Remove skillet from heat and top eggs with cheese. Transfer each egg with a scoop of salsa to a tortilla. Serves 2 to 4.

19

Tonya Sheppard
Galveston, TX

These are a favorite around my house...all the yummy ingredients for a great breakfast are wrapped up in a handy tortilla.

Bowl-Free Cereal-to-Go

1/4 c. sugar
1/2 t. cinnamon
1 c. bite-size crispy corn cereal
squares
1 c. bite-size crispy rice cereal
squares
1 c. bite-size crispy wheat cereal
squares
1 c. honey-nut doughnut-shaped
oat cereal
3/4 c. sliced almonds, toasted
1/3 c. butter, melted
1 c. dried banana chips
1/2 c. dried blueberries or raisins

In a small bowl, mix sugar and cinnamon; set aside. In a large, microwave-safe bowl, combine cereals and melted butter; toss until evenly coated. Microwave, uncovered, on high for 2 minutes, stirring after one minute. Stir in sugar mixture and banana chips until evenly coated. Microwave, uncovered, for one additional minute. Spread on wax paper to cool. Transfer to an airtight container; stir in blueberries or raisins. Makes 12 to 14 servings.

Amanda Pennings
Walla Walla, WA
Cereal without the milk!
A big handful of this and
I'm out the door, ready to
start my day.

Melon-Berry Bowls

1 honeydew melon, halved and
    seeded
6-oz. container favorite-flavor
    yogurt
1/2 c. blueberries
1 c. granola cereal

Use a melon baller to scoop
honeydew into balls. Combine
melon balls with remaining
ingredients. Spoon into individual
bowls to serve. Serves 2 to 4.

Jill Ball
Highland, UT
I am always looking for
quick, healthy and yummy
breakfast ideas for my
teenagers. This one has
become a favorite!

Steak & Egg Breakfast Burrito

2 frozen sliced sandwich steaks
4 eggs
2 T. milk
2 t. fresh chives, chopped
salt and pepper to taste
2 corn tortillas
salsa to taste
1/2 c. shredded Mexican-blend
   cheese, divided

In a skillet over medium heat, cook steaks until no longer pink; drain and set aside. Beat together eggs, milk, chives, salt and pepper. In same skillet, scramble eggs to desired doneness. Divide eggs evenly between tortillas; top each with steak, salsa and cheese. Roll up and microwave on high setting for 20 to 30 seconds to melt cheese. Makes 2 servings.

Shelly Turner
Boise, ID

Such a great way to enjoy classic steak and eggs when you're in a hurry!

Fruited Orange Yogurt

8-oz. container mascarpone
  cheese
32-oz. container plain yogurt
1/3 c. sugar
juice and zest of 2 oranges
Garnish: granola, blueberries,
  raspberries, sliced bananas

In a bowl, combine cheese, yogurt
and sugar. Stir in juice and zest.
Sprinkle granola over top. Serve
with fresh fruit. Serves 4 to 6.

23

Beth Bennett
Stratham, NH
A smooth and crunchy, sweet
and zingy breakfast you can
enjoy on the go.

Pigs in the Clover

14-3/4 oz. can creamed corn
2 to 3 potatoes, peeled, boiled
  and cubed
salt and pepper to taste
8 pork breakfast sausage links,
  browned

Pour creamed corn into a greased
8"x8" baking pan. Place potatoes
over corn; sprinkle with salt and
pepper. Arrange sausage links on top.
Cover with aluminum foil. Bake at
350 degrees for 30 minutes, or until
bubbly. Serves 4 to 6.

Cathy Nign
Temple City, CA

My Norwegian mother-in-law
gave me this recipe. She
told me this was a dish
she ate while growing up.

Breakfast Pizza

11-oz. tube refrigerated
   thin-crust pizza dough
14-oz. can pizza sauce
16-oz. container ricotta cheese
1/4 c. fresh oregano, chopped
favorite pizza toppings
4 eggs
salt and pepper to taste

Roll out dough into a 13-inch by 9-inch rectangle; transfer to a greased rimmed baking sheet. Spread pizza sauce on dough, leaving a 1/2-inch border. Top with cheese, oregano and other pizza toppings. Bake at 500 degrees for 4 to 5 minutes, or until crust begins to turn golden. Crack each egg into a small bowl and slip onto pizza, being careful not to break the yolks. Bake for another 5 minutes, until eggs are done as desired. Serves 2 to 4.

25

Connie Hilty
Pearland, TX

Is there anything better than pizza for breakfast?

Green Eggs & Ham

2 T. butter
1/2 c. fresh spinach
1 green onion, chopped
1/4 c. deli smoked ham, diced
3 eggs, beaten
2 T. pesto sauce
salt and pepper to taste

Melt butter in a skillet over medium heat. Cook spinach, green onion and ham in butter until warmed through and spinach is wilted, about 3 minutes. Add eggs to spinach mixture and cook until eggs start to set; stir in pesto, salt and pepper. Continue cooking until eggs reach desired doneness. Serves one to 2.

Chad Rutan
Gooseberry Patch

These are so good, I will eat them on a plane, on a train, on a boat, in a coat... anywhere, anytime!

PB&J Breakfast Bars

1-1/2 c. quick-cooking oats,
  uncooked
1/2 c. all-purpose flour
1/2 c. light brown sugar, packed
1/4 t. baking soda
1/4 t. plus 1/8 t. salt, divided
1/4 t. cinnamon
6 T. butter, melted
8-oz. pkg. cream cheese,
  softened
1/2 c. creamy peanut butter
1 egg, beaten
1/2 c. favorite-flavor jam

In a bowl, stir together oats, flour, brown sugar, baking soda, 1/4 teaspoon salt and cinnamon. Add melted butter and mix until crumbs form. Reserve 1/2 cup of oat mixture for topping; firmly spread remaining mixture in a lightly greased, parchment paper-lined 8"x8" baking pan. Bake at 350 degrees for 15 minutes, or until golden. In a bowl, beat together cream cheese, peanut butter, egg and remaining salt. Spread cream cheese mixture over baked crust; spread with jam. Top with reserved oat mixture. Bake for an additional 30 minutes, or until topping is golden; cool. Refrigerate for one hour, or until fully set. Cut into bars. Makes 12 to 15.

Angie Stewart Forester
Memphis, TN

This is our favorite quick breakfast item. My hubby can grab one of these as he walks out the door, because he always forgets to leave time for breakfast.

Lazy Man's Pancakes

3 T. butter
6 eggs
1-1/2 c. milk
1-1/2 c. all-purpose flour
3/4 t. salt
Optional: chopped walnuts,
  maple syrup

Melt butter in a 13"x9" baking pan
placed in a 425-degree oven.
Meanwhile, in a bowl, combine eggs,
milk, flour and salt; beat well. Slowly
pour mixture into buttered pan. Bake
at 425 degrees for 20 to 25 minutes,
until top is golden. Cut into squares;
serve topped with nuts and syrup,
if desired. Serves 5 to 6.

Mel Chencharick
Julian, PA

This is great when you're
pressed for time. No more
standing at the stove for an
hour flipping and frying...
just mix and pop in the oven.

Cranberry-Lime Cooler

6-oz. can frozen limeade
    concentrate, thawed
4 c. cold water
16-oz. bottle cranberry juice
    cocktail
1/4 c. orange drink mix
ice cubes
Garnish: fresh mint sprigs

Prepare limeade with water in a large
pitcher. Stir in cranberry juice and
orange drink mix. Pour over ice
cubes in tall mugs or glasses.
Garnish each with a sprig of mint.
Makes 8 servings.

29

**Ellie Brandel
Milwaukie, OR**

A refreshingly different
beverage to pair with
the rest of your
speedy breakfast.

Honey Crunch Granola

4 c. long-cooking oats, uncooked
1/2 c. unsalted slivered almonds
1/4 c. unsalted sunflower kernels
1/2 c. honey
1/2 c. butter
2 t. cinnamon
1/8 t. ground cloves
1 t. vanilla extract
1/8 t. salt

Mix oats, almonds and sunflower kernels in a large bowl; set aside. Combine honey, butter, spices, vanilla and salt in a microwave-safe bowl. Microwave on high setting until butter and honey are melted; stir well. Pour honey mixture over oat mixture; toss until well coated. Spread on a lightly greased 15"x10" jelly-roll pan. Bake at 350 degrees for 20 minutes, or until lightly golden. Allow to cool completely; store in an airtight container. Makes 8 servings.

Emily Hartzell
Portland, IN

For a delicious, healthy breakfast, serve over vanilla yogurt with fresh berries and bananas!

Sausage Muffins

1 lb. ground turkey sausage
1/4 c. butter
5-oz. jar sharp pasteurized
    process cheese spread
1/4 t. garlic powder
6 English muffins, split

In a skillet over medium heat, brown sausage; drain. Add butter, cheese and garlic powder; mix and cook until cheese melts. Spread sausage mixture on 6 English muffin halves. Place on an ungreased baking sheet and bake at 350 degrees for 15 minutes, or until heated through. Top with remaining halves of English muffins. Makes 6.

31

Carolyn Britton
Millry, AL

These are great to make ahead and freeze individually. Just heat and serve for a quick breakfast or snack.

Strawberry-Hazelnut Grits

3/4 c. quick-cooking grits,
   uncooked
1 T. butter
3 T. chocolate-hazelnut spread
6 to 7 strawberries, hulled and
   chopped

Prepare grits according to package
directions. Stir in butter and
chocolate-hazelnut spread. Fold in
strawberries. Serves 2.

Beth Kramer
Port Saint Lucie, FL

This combination of
strawberry, cocoa and
hazelnut is just too
yummy to pass up!

Barbara's Open-House Waffles

3 c. biscuit baking mix
1 c. millet flour
1/8 t. baking soda
1/4 c. canola oil
3 eggs, beaten
3 c. buttermilk
2 T. water
Garnish: maple syrup, fresh
  strawberries, whipped cream

In a bowl, whisk together baking mix, flour and baking soda. Add remaining ingredients except garnish and mix well. Drop batter by 1/2 cupfuls onto a heated waffle iron; cook according to manufacturer's directions. Top with maple syrup, strawberries and whipped cream. Serves 6 to 8.

33

Barbara McCurry
Carpinteria, CA

Every Saturday morning,
I serve these for family &
friends...it's fun, and the
neighbors love it!

Apple Breakfast Cobbler

4 apples, peeled, cored and
   sliced
1/4 c. honey
1 t. cinnamon
2 T. butter, melted
2 c. granola cereal
Garnish: milk or cream

Place apples in a slow cooker sprayed
with non-stick vegetable spray. In a
bowl, combine remaining ingredients
except garnish; sprinkle over apples.
Cover and cook on low setting for
7 to 9 hours, or on high setting for
3 to 4 hours. Garnish with milk or
cream. Serves 4.

Debi Gilpin
Sharpsburg, GA

What a fabulous slow-cooker
treat to wake up to on a
chilly winter morning!

Cranberry Hootycreek Pancakes

1/2 c. all-purpose flour
1/2 c. quick-cooking oats,
  uncooked
1 T. sugar
1 t. baking powder
1/2 t. baking soda
1/2 t. salt
1 t. vanilla extract
3/4 c. buttermilk
2 T. oil
1 egg, beaten
1/2 c. white chocolate chips
1/2 c. sweetened dried
  cranberries

35

In a bowl, mix flour, oats, sugar,
baking powder, baking soda and salt.
Add vanilla, buttermilk, oil and egg;
stir until well blended. Stir in white
chocolate chips and cranberries.
In a large, lightly greased griddle
over medium heat, drop batter by
1/4 cupfuls. Cook for about
3 minutes, until tops start to form
bubbles. Flip and cook 2 additional
minutes, or until both sides are
golden. Serves 4.

Sarah Lundvall
Ephrata, PA

This is my take on a
favorite cookie recipe...
for breakfast. My 2-year-old
gobbles them up faster
than I can make them.

Melt-In-Your-Mouth Biscuits

1-1/2 c. all-purpose flour
1/2 c. whole-wheat flour
4 t. baking powder
1/2 t. salt
2 T. sugar
1/4 c. chilled butter, sliced
1/4 c. shortening
2/3 c. milk
1 egg, beaten

In a large bowl, sift flours, baking powder, salt and sugar together; cut in butter and shortening. Add milk; stir in egg. Knead on a floured surface until smooth; roll out to 1/2-inch thickness. Cut with a biscuit cutter; place biscuits on ungreased baking sheets. Bake at 450 degrees for 10 to 15 minutes, until golden. Makes one to 2 dozen.

Sherri Hagel
Spokane, WA

Split and served with butter and jam or topped with sausage gravy, these flaky biscuits live up to their name!

Sausage Gravy

1 lb. ground pork breakfast
   sausage
1/4 c. all-purpose flour
3 to 4 c. milk
1/2 t. salt
1/4 t. pepper

Brown sausage in a large skillet over medium-high heat; do not drain. Stir in flour until mixture becomes thick. Reduce heat to medium-low. Gradually add milk, stirring constantly, until mixture reaches desired thickness. Season with salt and pepper. Serves 4 to 6.

37

Leslie Stimel
Columbus, OH

It's a snap to make this delicious homestyle gravy.

Bacon Griddle Cakes

12 slices bacon
2 c. pancake mix
Garnish: butter, maple syrup

On a griddle set to medium heat, cook bacon until crisp. Drain, reserving 2 tablespoons drippings. Meanwhile, prepare pancake mix according to package directions, omitting a little of the water or milk for a thicker batter. Arrange bacon slices 2 inches apart on griddle greased with reserved drippings. Slowly pour pancake batter over each piece of bacon, covering each slice. Cook until golden on both sides; serve with butter and maple syrup. Serves 4 to 6.

Joseph Drushal
Chicago, IL

So simple but so delicious! Why didn't I think of this sooner?

Texas Toads in the Hole

2 T. butter
4 slices Texas toast
4 eggs
salt and pepper to taste
Optional: jam, jelly or preserves

Spread butter on both sides of Texas toast. Using a biscuit cutter, cut a circle out of the middle of each slice of toast; set aside rounds. Place toast slices in a large, lightly greased skillet over medium heat; break an egg into each hole. Season with salt and pepper. Cook until egg white begins to set, then carefully flip. Continue to cook until eggs reach desired doneness. In a separate skillet, toast reserved bread rounds. Top rounds with jam, jelly or preserves, if desired. Serve with toast slices. Serves 4.

39

Elizabeth Holcomb
Canyon Lake, TX

I made this breakfast for my girls when they were little. They always loved it because of the funny name, as well as the fact they had eggs and toast all in one dish!

Scalloped Bacon & Eggs

1/4 c. onion, chopped
2 T. butter
2 T. all-purpose flour
1-1/2 c. milk
1 c. shredded Cheddar cheese
1/2 t. dry mustard
6 eggs, hard-boiled, peeled and
   sliced
1/2 t. salt
1/4 t. pepper
1-1/2 c. potato chips, crushed
10 slices bacon, crisply cooked
   and crumbled

In a skillet over medium heat, sauté onion in butter until translucent; stir in flour. Gradually add milk and cook, stirring constantly, until thickened. Add cheese and mustard, stirring until cheese melts. Place half the egg slices in a greased 8"x8" baking pan. Sprinkle with salt and pepper. Cover with half each of the cheese sauce, potato chips and bacon. Repeat layers. Bake, uncovered, at 350 degrees for 15 to 20 minutes. Serves 4 to 6.

Rita Morgan
Pueblo, CO

A few other ladies and I get together sometimes for brunch...I always bring this dish and they love it!

Bacon & Egg Potato Skins

2 baking potatoes
4 eggs, beaten
1 to 2 t. butter
salt and pepper to taste
1/4 c. shredded Monterey Jack
   cheese
1/4 c. shredded Cheddar cheese
4 slices bacon, crisply cooked
   and crumbled
Garnish: sour cream, chopped
   fresh chives

Bake potatoes at 400 degrees for one hour, until tender. Slice potatoes in half lengthwise; scoop out centers and reserve for another recipe. Place potato skins on a lightly greased baking sheet. Bake at 400 degrees for 6 to 8 minutes, until crisp. In a skillet over medium heat, scramble eggs in butter just until they begin to set. Add salt and pepper; remove from heat. Spoon equal amounts of eggs, cheeses and bacon into each potato skin. Reduce heat to 350 degrees and bake for 7 to 10 minutes, until cheese is melted and eggs are completely set. Garnish with sour cream and chives. Makes 4 servings.

41

Dale Duncan
Waterloo, IA

A tummy-filling
complete meal in a
potato skin...yummy!

Luscious Blueberry Syrup

1/2 c. sugar
1 T. cornstarch
1/3 c. water
2 c. fresh or frozen blueberries

In a saucepan over medium heat, combine sugar and cornstarch. Stir in water gradually. Add berries; bring to a boil. Boil, stirring constantly, for one minute, or until mixture thickens. Serve warm, or pour into a covered jar and keep in the refrigerator for several days. Makes about 2-1/2 cups.

Cindy Williams
Owensboro, KY

So quick & easy! It's delicious drizzled warm or cold over waffles, pancakes and even over ice cream or a slice of pound cake.

Blueberry-Lemon Crepes

3-oz. pkg. cream cheese,
   softened
1-1/2 c. half-and-half
1 T. lemon juice
3-3/4 pkg. instant lemon
   pudding mix
1/2 c. biscuit baking mix
1 egg
6 T. milk
1 c. blueberry pie filling

Combine cream cheese, half-and-half, lemon juice and dry pudding mix in a bowl. Beat with an electric mixer on low speed for 2 minutes. Refrigerate for 30 minutes. Lightly grease a 6" skillet and place over medium-high heat. In a bowl, combine biscuit baking mix, egg and milk. Beat until smooth. Pour 2 tablespoons of batter into skillet for each crepe. Rotating the skillet quickly, allow batter to cover the bottom of the skillet. Cook each crepe until lightly golden, then flip, cooking again until just golden. Spoon 2 tablespoonfuls of cream cheese mixture onto each crepe and roll up. Top with remaining cream cheese mixture and pie filling. Makes 6 servings.

Jo Ann
A scrumptious and
refreshing breakfast!

43

After-Church Egg Muffins

10-3/4 oz. can Cheddar cheese
  soup
1-1/2 c. milk
4 eggs
4 English muffins, split and
  toasted
3 T. butter, divided
4 slices Canadian bacon

In a bowl, mix together soup and milk. Fill 8 greased custard cups 1/2 full with soup mixture. Set cups on a baking sheet. Crack an egg into each cup, being careful not to break the yolks. Bake cups at 350 degrees for 12 minutes. Meanwhile, brown both sides of bacon in a skillet over medium heat. Top each muffin half with one teaspoon butter. Place 4 muffin halves on a baking sheet. Top each with a slice of bacon. Turn out a baked egg onto each bacon-topped muffin half. Drizzle remaining cheese sauce over each egg. Top with other halves of muffins. Bake for an additional 2 minutes, or until heated through. Makes 4 servings.

Megan Brooks
Antioch, TN

I whip these up for my boys almost every Sunday after church...they start asking for them right when we walk in the door.

Chocolate Chip-Pumpkin Waffles

1 egg, beaten
3/4 c. canned pumpkin
1/4 c. brown sugar, packed
1/4 c. butter, melted and slightly
    cooled
1-3/4 c. milk
1-1/2 c. all-purpose flour
1/2 c. whole-wheat flour
1 T. flax meal
1-1/2 t. pumpkin pie spice
1 T. baking powder
1/2 t. salt
1/2 c. semi-sweet chocolate chips
Optional: vanilla yogurt,
    cinnamon-sugar, toasted
    pumpkin seeds

In a bowl, whisk together egg,
pumpkin, brown sugar, butter and
milk. Add dry ingredients; whisk
well until smooth. Fold in chocolate
chips. Pour batter by 1/2 cupfuls into
a greased hot waffle iron. Cook
waffles according to manufacturer's
directions. Top waffles with a dollop
of yogurt, cinnamon-sugar and
pumpkin seeds, if desired. Serves 4.

45

Cindy Jamieson
Ontario, Canada

These taste wonderful,
and the kids are none
the wiser that they are
a tad healthier!

Sugarplum Bacon

1/2 c. brown sugar, packed
1 t. cinnamon
1/2 lb. bacon

In a bowl, combine brown sugar and cinnamon. Cut each bacon slice in half crosswise; dredge each slice in brown sugar mixture. Twist bacon slices and place in an ungreased 13"x9" baking pan. Bake at 350 degrees for 15 to 20 minutes, until bacon is crisp and sugar is bubbly. Place bacon on aluminum foil to cool. Serve at room temperature. Makes 8 servings.

Beth Burgmeier
East Dubuque, IL

Crunchy, sweet and salty... this bacon is out-of-this-world good! Cook some up for your brunch guests. They're sure to love it.

Farmers' Market Omelet

1 t. olive oil
1 slice bacon, diced
2 T. onion, chopped
2 T. zucchini, diced
5 cherry tomatoes, quartered
1/2 t. fresh thyme, minced
3 eggs, beaten
1/4 c. fontina cheese, shredded

Heat oil in a skillet over medium-high heat. Add bacon and onion; cook and stir until bacon is crisp and onion is tender. Add zucchini, tomatoes and thyme. Allow to cook until zucchini is soft and juice from tomatoes has slightly evaporated. Lower heat to medium and stir in eggs. Cook, lifting edges to allow uncooked egg to flow underneath. When eggs are almost fully cooked, sprinkle with cheese and fold over. Serves one.

47

Vickie

I love visiting the farmers' market bright & early on Saturday mornings... a terrific way to begin the day!

Scrambled Eggs & Lox

6 eggs, beaten
1 T. fresh dill, minced
1 T. fresh chives, minced
1 T. green onion, minced
pepper to taste
2 T. butter
4-oz. pkg. smoked salmon, diced

Whisk together eggs, herbs, onion and pepper. Melt butter in a large skillet over medium heat. Add egg mixture and stir gently with a spatula until eggs begin to set. Stir in salmon; continue cooking until eggs reach desired doneness. Serves 3.

Jackie Smulski
Lyons, IL

These eggs are sure to please everyone...they're excellent with toasted English muffins or bagels.

Orange-Cinnamon French Toast

2 to 4 T. butter, melted
2 T. honey
1/2 t. cinnamon
3 eggs, beaten
1/2 c. frozen orange juice
   concentrate, partially thawed
1/8 t. salt
6 slices French bread

Combine butter, honey and cinnamon together in a 13"x9" baking pan and set aside. Blend eggs, orange juice and salt together. Dip bread slices into egg mixture, coating both sides. Arrange dipped bread slices in baking pan. Bake, uncovered, at 400 degrees for 15 to 20 minutes, until golden. Serves 3 to 4.

49

Debra Fleischacker
Aurora, CO

Good recipes always get passed along, as this one will!

Eggs Benedict

8 slices Canadian bacon
1 t. lemon juice or vinegar
8 eggs
4 English muffins, split and
    toasted
3 T. butter, softened and divided
1 c. Hollandaise sauce, divided
3 T. fresh chives, chopped

Brown bacon in a skillet over
medium heat. Meanwhile, fill a large
saucepan with 2 inches of water and
lemon juice or vinegar; bring to a
simmer. Crack each egg into a
shallow bowl and slip them, one at a
time, into the water. Poach for about
3 minutes, until whites are set and
yolks are soft. Remove eggs with a
slotted spoon and drain on paper
towels. Top each toasted muffin half
with one teaspoon butter, one slice of
bacon, one egg and a drizzle of
Hollandaise sauce. Sprinkle with
chives. Serves 4.

Diana Chaney
Olathe, KS

Who knew a dish that looks
this elegant would be so
easy? Nothing beats these
eggs paired with a warm
cup of tea.

Spinach & Tomato French Toast

3 eggs
salt and pepper to taste
8 slices Italian bread
4 c. fresh spinach, torn
2 tomatoes, sliced
Garnish: grated Parmesan cheese

In a bowl, beat eggs with salt and
pepper. Dip bread slices into egg.
Place in a lightly greased skillet over
medium heat; cook one side until
lightly golden. Place fresh spinach
and two slices of tomato onto each
slice, pressing lightly to secure.
Flip and briefly cook on other side
until golden. Serves 4.

51

**Linda Bonwill
Englewood, FL**

A healthier way to make
French toast...plus,
it looks so pretty!

Granny Ruth's Chocolate Gravy

1 c. sugar
2 t. baking cocoa
1 t. cornstarch
1/2 c. milk
1 t. butter
1 t. vanilla extract

Mix together all ingredients in a saucepan over medium heat. Cook and stir until mixture reaches desired thickness. Serve warm. Makes about 6 servings.

Julie Marsh
Shelbyville, TN

This recipe is so special to our family...Granny Ruth made this for everyone. It is wonderful over hot biscuits!

Red Velvet Pancakes

1-1/2 c. all-purpose flour
2 T. baking cocoa
4 t. sugar
1-1/2 t. baking powder
1/2 t. baking soda
1 t. cinnamon
1 t. salt
2 eggs
1-1/4 c. buttermilk
1 T. red food coloring
1-1/2 t. vanilla extract
1/4 c. butter, melted
Optional: maple syrup, butter,
 whipped cream cheese

In a bowl, whisk together all dry ingredients. In a separate bowl, mix eggs, buttermilk, food coloring and vanilla. Add to dry ingredients and mix well. Fold in melted butter. Using an ice cream scoop, drop batter onto a lightly greased, hot griddle and cook until edges darken, about 5 minutes. Flip and cook until done. Serve topped with syrup and butter or whipped cream cheese. Makes one dozen pancakes.

53

Ashlee Haefs
Buna, TX

Red velvet cake is one of my family's favorites, so with this recipe we can have it for breakfast...what a great way to start the day!

Yummy Sausage Cups

1 lb. maple-flavored ground
 pork breakfast sausage
8-oz. pkg. shredded sharp
 Cheddar cheese
16-oz. container sour cream
1-oz. pkg. ranch salad dressing
 mix
4 2.1-oz. pkgs. frozen phyllo
 cups

Brown sausage in a skillet over
medium heat; drain and return to
skillet. Stir in remaining ingredients
except phyllo cups. Fill each phyllo
cup with a scoop of sausage mixture.
Arrange cups on ungreased baking
sheets. Bake at 350 degrees for
15 minutes, or until heated through
and cups are golden. Makes 5 dozen.

Angie Walsh
Cedar Rapids, IA

We enjoy having these
on Christmas day, but they're
good any time of year!
My mother-in-law makes them,
and they are a huge hit!

Sausage & Red Pepper Strata

6-oz. pkg. ground pork sausage
1/2 t. dried oregano
1/4 t. red pepper flakes
4 slices French bread, cubed
1/2 red pepper, diced
1 t. dried parsley
4 eggs
1 c. evaporated milk
1 t. Dijon mustard
1/4 t. pepper
1/2 c. shredded sharp Cheddar
   cheese

Brown sausage with oregano and red pepper flakes in a skillet over medium heat; drain and set aside. Line the bottom of a greased 8"x8" baking pan with bread; top with sausage mixture, red pepper and parsley. Set aside. Whisk together eggs, milk, mustard and pepper. Pour evenly over sausage mixture; cover tightly with aluminum foil and refrigerate 8 hours to overnight. Bake, covered with aluminum foil, at 350 degrees for 55 minutes. Remove foil; sprinkle with cheese and bake for an additional 5 minutes, or until cheese is melted. Serves 4 to 6.

55

Lynette Mull
Newton, KS

A delicious layered casserole you make the night before.

Sausage-Mozzarella Loaves

2 16-oz. loaves frozen bread
  dough, thawed
1 lb. ground pork sausage,
  browned and drained
12-oz. pkg. shredded mozzarella
  cheese
2 eggs, beaten
grated Parmesan cheese to taste

Roll bread loaves into two 16-inch by
8-inch rectangles. Sprinkle sausage
and mozzarella cheese over each
rectangle. Drizzle beaten eggs over
top. Top with Parmesan cheese. Roll
up each rectangle jelly-roll style,
starting at a short end. Place rolls
into 2 greased 9"x5" loaf pans,
seam-side down. Bake at 400 degrees
for 30 to 40 minutes, until tops are
golden. Serve warm. Makes 2 loaves.

Karen Carr
Elkins, WV

Golden bread loaves
filled with cheese and
sausage...yummy!

Puffy Pear Pancake

3 eggs, beaten
1 c. milk
1 t. vanilla extract
1 c. all-purpose flour
3 T. sugar
1/4 t. salt
4 pears, cored, peeled and sliced
1/4 c. brown sugar, packed
1/4 c. lemon juice

In a large bowl, whisk together eggs and milk. Add vanilla, flour, sugar and salt; whisk to combine. Pour batter into a large, ungreased oven-proof skillet. Bake at 425 degrees until golden and puffy, about 25 minutes. Meanwhile, combine pears, brown sugar and lemon juice in a bowl; stir well. Pour into a skillet over medium heat; sauté until pears are golden, about 5 minutes. Remove from heat. Spoon warm pear mixture over pancake before serving. Cut into wedges. Serves 4.

Jo Ann

Top each slice with a sprinkling of powdered sugar...yum!

Make-Ahead Breakfast Eggs

1 doz. eggs
1/2 c. milk
1/2 t. salt
1/4 t. pepper
1 T. butter
1 c. sour cream
12 slices bacon, crisply cooked
    and crumbled
1 c. shredded sharp Cheddar
    cheese

Beat together eggs, milk, salt and pepper; set aside. In a large skillet, melt butter over medium-low heat. Add egg mixture, stirring occasionally until eggs are set but still moist; remove from heat and cool. Stir in sour cream. Spread mixture in a greased shallow 2-quart casserole dish; top with bacon and cheese. Cover dish and refrigerate overnight. Uncover and bake at 300 degrees for 15 to 20 minutes, until heated through and cheese is melted. Serves 6 to 8.

Tamara Wallace
Roscoe, IL

For a wedding shower, my mom created a family cookbook... she asked everyone for special recipes and memories. This dish comes from that treasured collection.

Quick Strawberry Cream Danish

2 8-oz. pkgs. cream cheese,
  softened
1 egg, separated
1 t. vanilla extract
1 t. lemon juice
1 T. all-purpose flour
2 8-oz. tubes refrigerated
  crescent rolls
1/2 c. strawberry preserves,
  divided

Beat together cream cheese, egg
yolk, vanilla, lemon juice and flour.
Unroll and separate rolls; place a
teaspoon of cream cheese mixture
in the center of each triangle. Fold
over edges of rolls, leaving center
open. Brush with beaten egg white.
Place on ungreased baking sheets.
Bake at 350 degrees for 20 minutes.
Remove from oven and cool slightly.
Top each with a teaspoon of
strawberry preserves. Makes 16.

Beth Bundy
Long Prairie, MN

These are super easy, super
tasty and super pretty. A
couple of these with your
coffee will definitely make
your morning bright!

French Toast Casserole

1 c. brown sugar, packed
1/2 c. butter
2 c. corn syrup
1 loaf French bread, sliced
5 eggs, beaten
1-1/2 c. milk
1 t. vanilla extract
Garnish: powdered sugar, maple
   syrup

Melt together brown sugar, butter
and corn syrup in a saucepan over
low heat; pour into a greased
13"x9" baking pan. Arrange bread
slices over mixture and set aside.
Whisk together eggs, milk and vanilla;
pour over bread, coating all slices.
Cover and refrigerate overnight.
Uncover and bake at 350 degrees for
30 minutes, or until lightly golden.
Sprinkle with powdered sugar; serve
with warm syrup. Makes 6 to 8
servings.

Lori Hurley
Fishers, IN

A really simple way to make
French toast for a crowd.
Pop it in the fridge the
night before, then all you
have to do is bake it
in the morning!

Grandma's Warm Breakfast Fruit

3 apples, peeled, cored and
    thickly sliced
1 orange, peeled and sectioned
3/4 c. raisins
1/2 c. dried plums, chopped
3 c. plus 3 T. water, divided
1/2 c. sugar
1/2 t. cinnamon
2 T. cornstarch
Garnish: granola

Combine fruit and 3 cups water in
a saucepan over medium heat. Bring
to a boil; reduce heat and simmer
for 10 minutes. Stir in sugar and
cinnamon. In a small bowl, mix
together cornstarch and remaining
water; stir into fruit mixture. Bring
to a boil, stirring constantly; cook
and stir for 2 minutes. Spoon into
bowls; top with granola to serve.
Serves 6 to 8.

61

Virginia Watson
Scranton, PA
Keep this warm for brunch
in a mini slow cooker.

Best Brunch Casserole

4 c. croutons
2 c. shredded Cheddar cheese
8 eggs, beaten
4 c. milk
1 t. salt
1 t. pepper
2 t. mustard
1 T. dried, minced onion
6 slices bacon, crisply cooked
  and crumbled

Spread croutons in a greased
13"x9" baking pan; sprinkle with
cheese and set aside. In a bowl, whisk
together remaining ingredients
except bacon; pour over cheese.
Sprinkle bacon on top. Bake,
uncovered, at 325 degrees for 55 to
60 minutes, until set. Serves 8.

Lita Hardy
Santa Cruz, CA
My family & friends have
been enjoying this dish
for over 30 years!

Best-Ever Brunch Potatoes

2-1/2 lbs. redskin potatoes, diced
3 T. olive oil
8 eggs, beaten
1 t. salt
1/2 T. pepper
8 slices bacon, crisply cooked
   and crumbled
3/4 c. French onion dip
3/4 c. shredded sharp Cheddar
   cheese
1/2 c. green onions, chopped

In a skillet over medium heat, fry potatoes in oil until tender. In a separate lightly greased skillet, scramble eggs until fluffy; season with salt and pepper. Fold bacon, dip and cheese into potatoes; stir in scrambled eggs. Sprinkle green onions over top. Serves 6 to 8.

63

Gaybrielle Ray
Springfield, OH

I created this recipe by tossing together several of my favorite ingredients... it was a hit!

Sweet & Easy Iced Coffee

1/2 c. sweetened condensed milk,
   divided
4 c. strong brewed coffee, cooled
ice cubes

Place 2 tablespoons of sweetened
condensed milk into each of 4 tall
glasses. Pour one cup of cooled coffee
into each glass; stir to combine. Fill
glasses with ice; stir to chill. Serves 4.

Jen Licon-Conner
Gooseberry Patch

My love of iced coffee
started one summer when it
was just too hot for my
morning cup...now I make
it all year 'round!

Blueberry Pillows

8-oz. pkg. cream cheese,
  softened
16 slices Italian bread
1/2 c. blueberries
2 eggs, beaten
1/2 c. milk
1 t. vanilla extract

Spread cream cheese evenly on
8 bread slices; arrange blueberries
in a single layer over cream cheese.
Top with remaining bread slices,
gently pressing to seal; set aside.
Whisk together eggs, milk and vanilla
in a small bowl; brush over bread
slices. Arrange on a greased hot
griddle; cook until golden. Flip
and cook other side until golden.
Serves 8.

65

Kristie Rigo
Friedens, PA

A delightful blend of cream
cheese and blueberries
stuffed inside French toast.

Hashbrown Quiche

3 c. frozen shredded
   hashbrowns, thawed
1/4 c. butter, melted
3 eggs, beaten
1 c. half-and-half
3/4 c. cooked ham, diced
1/2 c. green onions, chopped
1 c. shredded Cheddar cheese
salt and pepper to taste

In an ungreased 9" pie plate, combine hashbrowns and butter. Press hashbrowns into the bottom and up the sides of the pie plate. Bake at 450 degrees for 20 to 25 minutes until, golden and crisp. Remove from oven and cool slightly. Meanwhile, combine remaining ingredients in a bowl. Pour mixture over hashbrowns. Lower oven temperature to 350 degrees; bake for 30 minutes, or until quiche is golden and set. Serves 4 to 6.

Sonya Labbe
Santa Monica, CA
The crust of this quiche is made with frozen hashbrowns. It is always a hit at family potlucks and brunches.

Dilled Crab Egg Cups

1/2 lb. crabmeat, flaked
8-oz. pkg. cream cheese, diced
1 T. fresh dill, chopped and
　　divided
1 doz. eggs
1/2 c. milk
1/2 c. sour cream
Optional: salad greens, favorite-
　　flavor salad dressing

Divide crabmeat and cream cheese
evenly among 12 greased muffin cups.
Sprinkle dill into each cup. In a
bowl, whisk together eggs, milk and
sour cream. Divide egg mixture
among muffin cups, filling each
about 3/4 full. Bake at 450 degrees
for 10 to 15 minutes, until puffed and
golden. Cool slightly; remove from
tin. Serve egg cups on a bed of salad
greens drizzled with dressing, if
desired. Makes one dozen.

67

Sandra Sullivan
Aurora, CO

A great dish for
pop-up brunches and
get-togethers.

Fiesta Corn Tortilla Quiche

1 lb. hot ground pork sausage
5 6-inch corn tortillas
4-oz. can chopped green chiles,
    drained
1 c. shredded Cheddar cheese
1 c. shredded Monterey Jack
    cheese
6 eggs, beaten
1/2 c. whipping cream
1/2 c. small-curd cottage cheese

Brown sausage in a skillet over medium heat; drain. Meanwhile, arrange tortillas in a lightly greased 9" pie plate, overlapping on the bottom and extending 1/2 inch over the edge of plate. Spoon sausage, chiles and cheeses into tortilla-lined pie plate. In a bowl, beat together remaining ingredients. Pour egg mixture over sausage mixture. Bake, uncovered, at 375 degrees for 45 minutes, or until golden. Cut into wedges to serve. Serves 4.

Vickie

I love that the crust of this quiche is made out of tortillas. Plus, it has a great spicy flavor, perfect for chilly mornings.

Breezy Brunch Skillet

6 slices bacon, diced
6 c. frozen diced potatoes
3/4 c. green pepper, chopped
1/2 c. onion, chopped
1 t. salt
1/4 t. pepper
6 eggs
1/2 c. shredded Cheddar cheese

In a large skillet over medium heat, cook bacon until crisp. Drain and set aside, reserving 2 T. drippings. In the same skillet, add potatoes, green pepper, onion, salt and pepper to drippings. Cook and stir for 2 minutes. Cover and cook for about 15 minutes, stirring occasionally, until potatoes are golden and tender. With a spoon, make 6 wells in potato mixture. Crack one egg into each well, taking care not to break the yolks. Cover and cook on low heat for 8 to 10 minutes, until eggs are completely set. Sprinkle with cheese and bacon. Serves 4 to 6.

69

Jill Ross
Gooseberry Patch

This one-skillet meal is a snap to toss together and the results are scrumptious. I'll even cook this up for dinner, it's so good!

Apple Walnut Coffee Cake

**Patty Sandness
Eastford, CT**

The chopped apple and walnuts really set this coffee cake apart. It has all the yummy flavors of apple pie, but in a cake!

3 eggs, beaten
1 c. oil
2 c. sugar
1 T. vanilla extract
3 c. all-purpose flour
1 t. salt
1/2 t. baking powder
1 t. baking soda
3/4 t. nutmeg
1 T. cinnamon
2 c. apples, peeled, cored and
    chopped
1 c. chopped walnuts

In a bowl, combine all ingredients except apple and nuts; mix well. Stir in apple and nuts; pour into greased and floured Bundt® pan. Bake at 300 degrees for 45 minutes. Increase heat to 325 degrees and bake an additional 20 minutes. Cool on a wire rack for 20 minutes; turn out onto a serving plate. Top with Glaze before serving. Serves 16.

Glaze:

1 c. powdered sugar
1-1/2 T. milk
1/2 t. vanilla

In a bowl, whisk together all ingredients.

Cranberry-Orange Warmer

16-oz. pkg. frozen cranberries,
  thawed
4-inch cinnamon stick
8 c. water
6-oz. can frozen orange juice
  concentrate, thawed
6-oz. can frozen lemonade
  concentrate, thawed
1 c. sugar

In a saucepan, bring cranberries,
cinnamon stick and water to a boil.
Boil for 5 minutes. Strain, discarding
cranberries and cinnamon stick.
Return juice to saucepan. Add juice
concentrates and sugar to saucepan;
stir until sugar melts. Serve warm.
Makes 20 servings.

71

Della Feist
Faith, SD

This is a favorite drink
around our home during the
fall and winter holidays.
Make a double batch and
invite friends over.

Sausage-Cranberry Quiche

1/2 lb. sage-flavored ground
  pork sausage
1/4 c. onion, chopped
3/4 c. sweetened dried
  cranberries
9-inch pie crust
1-1/2 c. shredded Monterey Jack
  cheese
3 eggs, beaten
1-1/2 c. half-and-half

In a large skillet over medium-high heat, brown sausage with onion; drain. Remove from heat and stir in cranberries. Line a 9" pie plate with pie crust. Sprinkle cheese into crust; evenly spoon in sausage mixture. In a bowl, combine eggs and half-and-half; whisk until mixed but not frothy. Pour egg mixture over sausage mixture. Bake at 375 degrees for 40 to 45 minutes, until a knife inserted in the center comes out clean. Let stand for 10 minutes before serving. Makes 6 servings.

Wanda Closs
Mount Airy, MD

The tartness of cranberries combined with spicy sausage makes a terrific match!

Pennsylvania Dutch Scrapple

1 lb. boneless pork loin, chopped
1 c. cornmeal
14-1/2 oz. can chicken broth
1/4 t. dried thyme
1/4 t. salt
1/2 c. all-purpose flour
1/4 t. pepper
2 T. oil
Optional: maple syrup

In a saucepan, cover pork with water; bring to a boil over medium heat. Simmer until fork-tender, about an hour; drain. Process in a food processor until minced. In a large saucepan over medium heat, combine pork, cornmeal, broth, thyme and salt; bring to a boil. Reduce heat and simmer, stirring constantly, for 2 minutes, or until mixture is very thick. Line a 9"x5" loaf pan with wax paper, letting paper extend above top of pan. Spoon pork mixture into pan; cover and chill for 4 hours to overnight. Unmold; cut into slices and set aside. On a plate, combine flour and pepper. Coat slices with flour mixture. In a large skillet, heat oil over medium heat; cook slices on both sides until golden. Drizzle with syrup, if desired. Serves 12.

73

Virginia Watson
Scranton, PA

Squares of this savory dish are usually served for breakfast...but sometimes, it's great for dinner too.

Cathy's Scotch Eggs

1 lb. ground pork sausage
2 T. dried parsley
1/2 t. dried sage
1/2 t. dried thyme
8 eggs, hard-boiled and peeled
1/2 c. all-purpose flour
1/2 t. salt
1/4 t. pepper
2 eggs, lightly beaten
1-1/2 c. dry bread crumbs
oil for frying
Optional: mustard

Combine sausage and herbs; mix well. Divide into 8 patties. Cover each hard-boiled egg with a sausage patty, pressing to cover and seal. Combine flour, salt and pepper. Roll eggs in flour mixture, then in beaten eggs and bread crumbs. Heat one inch of oil in a saucepan over medium-high heat. Cook eggs, a few at a time, in hot oil for 10 minutes, or until golden on all sides. Drain; chill in refrigerator. Slice into halves or quarters. Serve chilled with mustard, if desired. Serves 8.

Jamie Wyatt
Fayetteville, GA
My husband and I fell in love with Scotch Eggs while visiting England in 1980. Upon our return, my cousin shared her family recipe with us!

Southern Veggie Brunch Casserole

Jennifer McClure
Lebanon, IN

Our family always has this breakfast dish for dinner, and it's fondly called "brinner" by our two children.

1 lb. ground pork sausage,
   browned and drained
1/2 c. green onions, chopped
1 green pepper, diced
1 red pepper, diced
1 jalapeño pepper, seeded and
   diced
2 tomatoes, chopped
2 c. shredded mozzarella cheese
1 c. biscuit baking mix
1 doz. eggs, beaten
1 c. milk
1/2 t. dried oregano
1/2 t. salt
1/4 t. pepper

In a greased 3-quart casserole dish, layer sausage, onions, peppers, tomatoes and cheese. In a large bowl, whisk together remaining ingredients; pour over cheese. Bake, uncovered, at 350 degrees for 55 to 60 minutes, until set and top is golden. Let stand for 10 minutes before serving. Serves 6 to 8.

Country Cabin Potatoes

4 14-1/2 oz. cans sliced potatoes, drained
2 10-3/4 oz. cans cream of celery soup
16-oz. container sour cream
10 slices bacon, crisply cooked and crumbled
6 green onions, thinly sliced

Place potatoes in a slow cooker. In a bowl, combine remaining ingredients; pour over potatoes and stir gently. Cover and cook on high setting for 4 to 5 hours. Makes 10 to 12 servings.

Carol Lytle
Columbus, OH

One fall, we stayed in a beautiful 1800s log cabin in southern Ohio. Not only was it peaceful and relaxing, but breakfast was brought to us each morning...what a treat!

Sausage Breakfast Bake

1 lb. hot ground pork sausage
28-oz. pkg. frozen hashbrowns
   with onions and peppers,
   thawed
1 c. sliced mushrooms
2 c. shredded Monterey Jack
   cheese
10 eggs
1/2 c. milk
salt and pepper to taste

In a skillet over medium heat, brown sausage; drain. In a large bowl, combine sausage, hashbrowns, mushrooms and cheese. Spread evenly in a greased 13"x9" baking pan. Beat together eggs, milk, salt and pepper. Pour egg mixture over hashbrown mixture. Cover with aluminum foil and bake at 375 degrees for one hour. Remove foil and continue baking for an additional 15 minutes, or until golden. Serves 8.

Roxanne Sulzbach
Akron, OH

This tasty bake can be made ahead and warmed for a quick breakfast...my husband and son love it!

Tex-Mex Egg Puff

1 doz. eggs, beaten
2 4-oz. cans chopped green
   chiles, drained
1/2 c. butter, melted and cooled
   slightly
1/2 c. all-purpose flour
1 t. baking powder
1/2 t. salt
16-oz. pkg. shredded Monterey
   Jack cheese
16-oz. container small-curd
   cottage cheese

In a large bowl, whisk together all
ingredients. Spoon into a greased
13"x9" baking pan. Bake, uncovered,
at 350 degrees for 35 to 40 minutes,
until set. Cut into squares. Serves 8
to 10.

Carol Creed
Battlefield, MO

I experimented with the
ingredients until this recipe
was just right! Mix, bake
and serve. How easy is that?

Mom's Cheesy Hashbrowns

1/4 c. butter
1 sweet onion, chopped
2 c. shredded Cheddar cheese
1 c. sour cream
30-oz. pkg. frozen country-style
  shredded hashbrowns, thawed

Melt butter in a saucepan over
medium heat. Add onion and cook
until translucent, about 5 minutes.
Mix in cheese and continue stirring
until melted. Remove from heat; stir
in sour cream. Gently fold mixture
into hashbrowns. Spoon into a
greased 2-quart casserole dish. Bake,
uncovered, at 350 degrees for 60 to
75 minutes, until heated through and
top is golden. Serves 6 to 8.

79

Valerie Hendrickson
Cedar Springs, MI

My mother used to make
this scrumptious dish
the old-fashioned way. My
version is simplified, yet
is still full of hearty
homestyle flavor!

Easy Breakfast Squares

24-oz. pkg. frozen shredded
   hashbrowns
1-1/2 c. shredded mozzarella
   cheese
1-1/2 c. shredded Cheddar
   cheese
1 onion, diced
2 c. cooked ham, diced
salt and pepper to taste
3 eggs
1 c. milk

In a lightly greased 13"x9" baking pan,
layer hashbrowns, cheeses, onion and
ham; season with salt and pepper. Set
aside. In a bowl, beat together eggs
and milk; pour over ham. Cover;
refrigerate 8 hours to overnight.
Uncover; bake at 350 degrees for
45 minutes. Cut into squares to
serve. Serves 6 to 8.

Vicki Hirsch
Platteville, WI

This overnight dish is
filled with all your
breakfast favorites!

Mexican Brunch Casserole

2 4-oz. cans whole green chiles,
   drained
2 to 3 tomatoes, chopped
2 c. shredded Colby Jack cheese
1 c. biscuit baking mix
3 eggs
1 c. milk
1/2 t. salt

In a lightly greased 8"x8" baking pan,
layer chiles, tomatoes and cheese.
Beat together remaining ingredients
and spoon over cheese. Bake,
uncovered, at 375 degrees for 30 to
35 minutes, until set. Serves 3 to 4.

81

Olive Herzberg
Lomita, CA

This is a great brunch
dish...it's got yummy
Mexican flavors that are
sure to have you coming
back for seconds.

Mushroom & Sausage Mini Quiches

8-oz. pkg. breakfast turkey
   sausage links, sliced
1 t. olive oil
8-oz. can sliced mushrooms
1/4 c. green onions, sliced
1/4 c. shredded Swiss cheese
1 t. pepper
5 eggs
3 egg whites
1 c. milk

Brown sausage in a skillet over medium-high heat; drain and transfer to a bowl. To the same skillet, add oil and mushrooms. Cook, stirring often, until golden, about 5 to 7 minutes. Add mushrooms to sausage. Stir in green onions, cheese and pepper. In a separate bowl, whisk together eggs, egg whites and milk. Divide egg mixture evenly among 12 lightly greased muffin cups. Sprinkle a heaping tablespoon of sausage mixture into each cup. Bake at 325 degrees for 25 minutes, or until tops are golden. Remove from cups; cool on a wire rack. Makes one dozen.

Rebecca Payerle
Dublin, OH

These mini quiches are so tasty and simple. Sometimes I whip them up and take them to work for my coworkers... they love them!

Maple-Pecan Brunch Ring

3/4 c. chopped pecans
1/2 c. brown sugar, packed
2 t. cinnamon
2 17.3-oz. tubes refrigerated
   jumbo flaky biscuits
2 T. butter, melted
1/2 c. maple syrup

Combine pecans, brown sugar and cinnamon; set aside. Split each biscuit horizontally; brush half of the biscuits with butter and sprinkle with half the pecan mixture. Arrange topped biscuits in a circle on an ungreased baking sheet; overlap each biscuit slightly and keep within 2 inches of the edge of the baking sheet. Brush remaining biscuit halves with butter; sprinkle with remaining pecan mixture. Arrange a second ring just inside the first ring, overlapping edges. Bake at 350 degrees for 30 to 35 minutes, until golden. Remove to wire rack; cool 10 minutes. Brush with maple syrup. Makes about 12 servings.

83

Leslie Williams
Americus, GA

A sweet & simple way to make
a tasty treat for guests.

Aunt Kornye's Cinnamon Rolls

Ruby Kelsey
Holts Summit, MO

This recipe was found in my
great-great-aunt Kornye's
handwritten recipe book.
At the bottom of the card
she wrote "May increase
waist size."

3 envs. active dry yeast
2-1/2 c. warm water
4-1/2 c. all-purpose flour
18-1/2 oz. pkg. white cake mix
powdered sugar for dusting
1 c. butter, softened
1 c. brown sugar, packed
1/4 c. cinnamon
16-oz. container cream
   cheese icing

Dissolve yeast in very warm water,
110 to 115 degrees. Add flour and dry
cake mix; stir and knead until
smooth. Transfer to a greased bowl;
cover with a tea towel and let rise
until double in bulk, about
1-1/2 hours. Punch dough down,
cover and let rise again until double
in bulk, another hour. Roll out
dough 1/2-inch thick on a surface
dusted with powdered sugar; cut into
2 rectangles. Combine butter, brown
sugar and cinnamon; spread equally
over each rectangle. Roll up jelly-roll
style, starting with a long end. Slice
into 2-inch-thick slices. Place on a
greased baking sheet and let rise for
30 minutes. Bake at 375 degrees for
20 minutes, or until golden. Cool
slightly; spread with icing. Makes 10
to 15.

Apple Jack Muffins

2-1/3 c. all-purpose flour
1 c. plus 3 T. sugar, divided
1 T. baking powder
4 t. cinnamon, divided
1 t. baking soda
1/2 t. salt
1-1/2 c. apples, peeled, cored
   and finely chopped
1 c. buttermilk
1/3 c. milk
1/3 c. ricotta cheese
3 T. oil
1 T. vanilla extract
2 egg whites
1 egg, beaten

In a large bowl, sift together flour,
one cup sugar, baking powder,
2 teaspoons cinnamon, baking soda
and salt. Fold in apples; stir, then
make a well in the center. Whisk
together remaining ingredients;
pour into well in flour mixture.
Gently stir until just moistened.
Spoon batter equally into 18 greased
muffin cups. Combine remaining
sugar and cinnamon; sprinkle evenly
over batter. Bake at 400 degrees for
18 minutes, or until a toothpick
inserted in a muffin tests clean.
Makes 1-1/2 dozen.

85

Zoe Bennett
Columbia, SC

The best combination...
apples and cinnamon!

Blueberry Oatmeal Crisp

4 c. blueberries
1 c. all-purpose flour, divided
3/4 c. brown sugar, packed
3/4 c. long-cooking oats,
  uncooked
1/2 t. cinnamon
1/4 t. nutmeg
5 to 6 T. butter

Combine blueberries with 1/4 cup flour in a greased 11"x7" baking pan; mix thoroughly. In a bowl, combine remaining flour and other ingredients except butter. Cut in butter until coarse crumbs form; sprinkle over blueberries. Bake at 350 degrees for 25 minutes, or until top is golden and blueberries are bubbly. Makes 6 to 8 servings.

Amy Bastian
Mifflinburg, PA

This crisp is perfect on a brisk fall morning. Paired with some hot tea, it'll keep you warm and full all day!

Hot Chocolate Muffins

1/2 c. butter, softened
1 c. sugar
4 eggs, separated
6 T. hot chocolate mix
1/2 c. boiling water
2/3 c. milk
3 c. all-purpose flour
2 T. baking powder
1 t. salt
2 t. vanilla extract

Blend butter and sugar together in a large bowl; add egg yolks and beat until well mixed. In a separate bowl, dissolve hot chocolate mix in boiling water; add to butter mixture along with milk. Sift together flour, baking powder and salt; add to butter mixture. In a separate bowl, beat egg whites with an electric mixer on high speed until stiff peaks form; fold egg whites and vanilla into mixture. Pour into greased muffin tins until 3/4 full. Bake at 375 degrees for 20 to 25 minutes, until centers test done with a toothpick. Makes 1-1/2 to 2 dozen.

87

Carol Hickman
Kingsport, TN

A tasty breakfast treat for all the chocolate lovers out there!

Potato Doughnuts

2 envs. active dry yeast
1/2 c. warm water
1 c. sugar
3/4 c. shortening
1-1/2 c. mashed potatoes
3 eggs, beaten
2 c. milk
1 T. salt
1 T. lemon extract
6 to 8 c. all-purpose flour
oil for frying
Garnish: cinnamon-sugar,
    powdered sugar

Dissolve yeast in very warm water, 110 to 115 degrees; set aside. In a separate bowl, blend together sugar and shortening. Add potatoes, eggs, milk, salt, lemon extract and yeast mixture; mix well. Add in flour; mix and knead well until a soft dough forms. Place dough in a greased bowl; cover with a tea towel and let rise in a warm place until double in size, about one hour. Roll out dough 1/2-inch thick; cut with a doughnut cutter. Let doughnuts rise, uncovered, about 30 minutes. In a deep saucepan, heat several inches of oil to 375 degrees. Fry doughnuts, a few at a time, until golden; drain. Sprinkle with cinnamon-sugar or powdered sugar. Makes 4 dozen.

Emily Oravecz
New York, NY

What's better than a warm doughnut and a hot cup of coffee? These are also a great way to use up leftover mashed potatoes.

Cherry Turnovers

17-1/4 oz. pkg. frozen puff
    pastry, thawed
21-oz. can cherry pie filling,
    drained
1 c. powdered sugar
2 T. water

Separate puff pastry sheets and cut each into 4 squares. Divide pie filling evenly among squares. Brush pastry edges with water and fold in half diagonally. Seal and crimp edges with a fork. With a knife, make a small slit in tops of turnovers to vent. Bake on an ungreased baking sheet at 400 degrees for 15 to 18 minutes, until puffed and golden. Let cool slightly. Blend together powdered sugar and water; drizzle over warm turnovers. Makes 8.

Lynda Robson
Boston, MA

These are so quick & easy
but taste like you spent
hours in the kitchen
making them!

Peanut Butter Crunch Coffee Cake

1 t. cinnamon
1-1/4 c. sugar, divided
1/2 c. butter, softened
1 c. sour cream
1 t. vanilla extract
2 eggs
2 c. all-purpose flour
1-1/2 t. baking powder
1 t. baking soda
1/4 t. salt
1/4 c. chopped pecans
4 chocolate-covered crispy
   peanut butter candy bars,
   crushed

Mix together cinnamon and 1/4 cup sugar; set aside. In a bowl, beat 1/2 cup butter until creamy. Beat in sour cream, vanilla and eggs. In a separate bowl, combine flour, baking powder, baking soda, remaining sugar and salt. Add to butter mixture; mix thoroughly. Spoon half the batter into a greased 8"x8" baking pan. Sprinkle with half each of the cinnamon-sugar, pecans and crushed candy bars. Pour remaining batter into pan; top with the remaining cinnamon-sugar, pecans and crushed candy bars. Bake at 325 degrees for 45 minutes. Cool in pan on a wire rack for 15 minutes. Makes 8 to 10 servings.

Pat Minnich
El Cajon, CA

This much-loved recipe has never been published before, but it did win an award at the county fair.

Cinnamon Cream Cheese Squares

2 8-oz. tubes refrigerated
  crescent rolls
8-oz. pkg. cream cheese,
  softened
1 t. vanilla extract
1/2 c. sugar
1/4 c. butter, melted
cinnamon-sugar to taste

Unroll one tube of crescent rolls
and arrange in a lightly greased
13"x9" baking pan; pinch seams
together. In a bowl, beat together
cream cheese, vanilla and sugar;
spread over rolls in pan. Top with
remaining tube of crescent rolls,
pinching together seams. Drizzle
melted butter over top layer of
crescents and sprinkle with
cinnamon-sugar. Bake at 350 degrees
for 30 minutes, or until golden.
Serves 10 to 12.

Jody Geary
Rockland, MA
I am asked to make these no
matter where I go! They're
scrumptious warm or cold.

Banana Chocolate-Toffee Drop Scones

2-1/2 c. biscuit baking mix
1/2 c. semi-sweet chocolate chips
1/2 c. toffee baking bits
1/4 c. plus 2 T. sugar, divided
1/4 c. whipping cream
1/2 t. vanilla extract
1 egg, beaten
3/4 c. ripe banana, mashed
1 T. milk

In a bowl, stir together baking mix, chocolate chips, toffee bits, 1/4 cup sugar, whipping cream, vanilla, egg and banana until a soft dough forms. Drop dough by 10 heaping tablespoonfuls onto greased baking sheets. Brush tops of scones with milk; sprinkle with remaining sugar. Bake at 425 degrees for 11 to 13 minutes, until golden. Makes 10.

Karen Puchnick
Butler, PA

There's something about the taste of banana and chocolate that just can't be beat... these scones capture that flavor perfectly.

Fresh Strawberry Bread

3 c. all-purpose flour
2 c. sugar
1-1/2 t. cinnamon
1 t. baking soda
1 t. salt
1 c. oil
4 eggs, beaten
2 c. strawberries, hulled and
    diced
Optional: 1-1/4 c. chopped nuts

In a bowl, combine flour, sugar,
cinnamon, baking soda and salt.
In a separate bowl, blend together
oil and eggs; fold in strawberries.
Gradually add egg mixture into flour
mixture; stir until just moistened.
Add nuts, if using. Pour into 2
greased and floured 9"x5" loaf pans.
Bake at 350 degrees for one hour.
Makes 2 loaves.

Mary Patenaude
Griswold, CT

A slice of this bread is
delicious served with
a dab of cream cheese or
homemade strawberry jam.

Ginger & Currant Scones

1 egg, beaten
3 T. brown sugar, packed
1 t. rum or rum-flavored extract
1 t. baking powder
2 T. milk
1 c. all-purpose flour
1/4 c. butter, softened
3/4 c. currants
2 T. candied ginger, chopped

In a large bowl, mix together all ingredients until well blended. Divide dough into 8 to 10 balls; flatten. Arrange scones on ungreased baking sheets. Bake at 350 degrees for 15 minutes, or until golden. Makes 8 to 10.

Selma Cherkas
Worcester, MA
The candied ginger adds a spicy sweetness to these scones that goes so well with the currants.

Monkey Bread

1/2 c. sugar
1-1/2 t. cinnamon
3 12-oz. tubes refrigerated
   biscuits, quartered
1 c. brown sugar, packed
1/2 c. butter, melted
2 T. water

Combine sugar and cinnamon in
a bowl. Roll biscuit pieces in sugar
mixture; place in a greased Bundt®
pan. Combine brown sugar, butter
and water; pour over biscuits. Bake at
350 degrees for 30 minutes. Invert
onto a serving plate. Serves 6 to 8.

95

Michelle Pettit
Sebree, KY

This scruptious dish is
always a big hit. I usually
have to make two batches
because someone will always
try to sneak away with one
to take home!

Raised Doughnuts

2 c. boiling water
1/2 c. sugar
1 T. salt
2 T. shortening
2 envs. active dry yeast
2 eggs, beaten
7 c. all-purpose flour
oil for frying
Garnish: additional sugar for
    coating

Stir water, sugar, salt and shortening together in a large bowl; sprinkle yeast on top. Set aside; cool to room temperature. Blend in eggs; gradually add flour. Cover and let rise until double in bulk. Roll out dough 1/2-inch thick; cut with a doughnut cutter. Cover doughnuts and let rise until double in bulk, about 1-1/2 hours. In a deep saucepan, heat several inches of oil to 360 degrees. Fry doughnuts, a few at a time, until golden; drain. Spoon sugar into a paper bag; add doughnuts and shake to coat. Makes about 4 dozen.

Pam James
Delaware, OH

Every Tuesday night while I was growing up, my grandmother would make this dough for homemade doughnuts...even now, nothing compares to them.

Overnight Caramel Pecan Rolls

2 3.4-oz. pkgs. instant
   butterscotch pudding mix
1 c. brown sugar, packed
1 c. chopped pecans
1/2 c. chilled butter
36 frozen rolls, divided

Combine dry pudding mixes, brown sugar and pecans in a bowl. Cut in butter; set aside. Arrange half the frozen rolls in a lightly greased Bundt® pan. Sprinkle half the pudding mixture over top. Repeat layering with remaining rolls and pudding mixture. Cover loosely; refrigerate overnight. Bake at 350 degrees for one hour. Invert onto a serving plate. Serves 10 to 12.

Laura Carter
Vinita, OK

I got this recipe from my grandmother and mother... it's a family favorite that we all enjoy.

Cranberry-Orange Scones

**Dayna Hansen
Junction City, OR**

My sisters and I always gather for an annual "sisters brunch." We each share special moments, gifts and yummy dishes. These scones are a favorite!

2 c. all-purpose flour
10 t. sugar, divided
1 T. orange zest
1/4 t. baking soda
2 t. baking powder
1/2 t. salt
1/3 c. chilled butter, sliced
1 c. sweetened dried cranberries
1/4 c. plus 1 T. orange juice,
  divided
1/4 c. half-and-half
1 egg, beaten
1 T. milk
1/2 c. powdered sugar

Combine flour, 7 teaspoons sugar, orange zest, baking soda, baking powder and salt; cut in butter until coarse crumbs form. In a small bowl, stir together cranberries, 1/4 cup orange juice, half-and-half and egg. Add to flour mixture and mix until a soft dough forms. Knead 6 to 8 times on a lightly floured surface; pat into an 8-inch circle. Cut into 8 wedges; separate wedges and place on an ungreased baking sheet. Brush with milk; sprinkle with remaining sugar. Bake at 400 degrees for 12 to 15 minutes; cool slightly. Combine powdered sugar and remaining orange juice; drizzle over warm scones. Makes 8.

Sweet Twists

1 env. active dry yeast
1/4 c. warm water
3-3/4 c. all-purpose flour
1-1/2 t. salt
1 c. butter
2 eggs, beaten
1/2 c. sour cream
3 t. vanilla extract, divided
1-1/2 c. sugar

Dissolve yeast in very warm water, 110 to 115 degrees; set aside. Mix flour and salt in a large bowl; cut in butter until coarse crumbs form. Blend in eggs, sour cream, one teaspoon vanilla and yeast mixture; cover and chill overnight. Combine sugar and remaining vanilla. Sprinkle 1/2 cup vanilla-sugar mixture on a flat surface; roll out dough into a 16-inch by 8-inch rectangle. Sprinkle one tablespoon of vanilla-sugar mixture over dough; fold dough over and roll into a rectangle again. Continue sprinkling mixture, folding and rolling until no vanilla-sugar remains. Cut dough into 4-inch by 1-inch strips; twist strips and place on greased baking sheets. Bake at 350 degrees for 15 to 20 minutes. Makes 2 dozen.

Mary Jane Tolman
Rocky Mount, NC

These go great with a tall glass of cold milk for dunking.

Sweet Berry Popover

1 c. milk
1 T. butter, melted
1/2 t. vanilla extract
1/4 c. plus 1 T. sugar, divided
1/4 t. salt
1/8 t. nutmeg
1 c. all-purpose flour
2 eggs, beaten
1 c. berries
1/4 t. cinnamon

In a large bowl, whisk together milk, butter, vanilla, 1/4 cup sugar, salt and nutmeg; blend in flour. Gradually mix in eggs; set aside. Butter a 9" pie plate; add berries in a single layer into center of plate. Gently pour batter on top. Combine remaining sugar with cinnamon; sprinkle over batter. Bake at 450 degrees for 20 minutes. Lower heat to 350 degrees; continue baking until popover is golden, about 20 additional minutes. Slice into wedges; serve immediately. Makes 8 servings.

Elisabeth Macmillan
British Columbia, Canada
Use the freshest berries of the season for a deliciously different breakfast.

Morning Glory Muffins

2 c. all-purpose flour
1-1/4 c. sugar
2 t. baking soda
2 t. cinnamon
1/2 t. salt
2 c. carrots, peeled and grated
1/2 c. raisins
1/2 c. chopped pecans
3 eggs, beaten
1 c. oil
1 apple peeled, cored and
   shredded
2 t. vanilla extract

In a large bowl, combine flour, sugar, baking soda, cinnamon and salt. Stir in carrots, raisins and pecans. In a separate bowl, combine eggs, oil, apple and vanilla. Add egg mixture to flour mixture; stir until just combined. Spoon into greased or paper-lined muffin cups, filling 3/4 full. Bake at 350 degrees for 15 to 18 minutes, until golden. Makes 1-1/2 dozen.

Violet Leonard
Chesapeake, VA
These muffins are fantastic and filling. You can keep them in the freezer and thaw as needed.

Homemade Bagels

1 env. active dry yeast
1 c. warm water
2 T. sugar
1-1/2 t. salt
2-3/4 c. all-purpose flour,
    divided
Garnish: favorite-flavor cream
    cheese

In a large bowl, dissolve yeast in very warm water, 110 to 115 degrees. Add sugar, salt and half the flour to the yeast mixture; mix until smooth. Stir in remaining flour. Knead dough for 10 minutes on a lightly floured surface. Cover and let rise in a warm place until double in bulk. Punch down and divide into 8 equal pieces. Form each piece into a doughnut shape; let rise for 20 minutes. Bring a large pot of water to a boil; add bagels and boil for 7 minutes, turning once. Remove from water and place on a greased baking sheet. Bake at 375 degrees for 30 to 35 minutes, until golden. Cool slightly; slice and top with cream cheese. Makes 8 bagels.

Phyllis Peters
Three Rivers, MI

My daughter-in-law shared this recipe...the bagels are simple to make and so good.

Spiced Zucchini Bars

2 c. all-purpose flour
2 t. baking soda
1/2 t. salt
2 t. cinnamon
3 eggs, beaten
1 c. oil
2 c. sugar
1 t. vanilla extract
1 t. lemon juice
1 c. raisins
2 c. zucchini, grated
3/4 c. chopped nuts
16-oz. container cream cheese
   icing

In a bowl, combine flour, baking soda, salt and cinnamon; set aside. In a separate bowl, whisk together eggs, oil, sugar, vanilla and lemon juice. Gradually add flour mixture to egg mixture. Fold in remaining ingredients except frosting; pour into a greased and floured 15"x10" jelly-roll pan. Bake at 325 degrees for 25 to 35 minutes, until lightly golden. Cool; spread with icing. Cut into bars. Makes 3 dozen.

Erin Carnes
Gaines, MI

These yummy bars are one of the first treats I make when the zucchini is ready to pick in my garden.

Lemon Coffee Cake

1 c. chopped walnuts
1/2 c. sugar
2 t. cinnamon
18-1/4 oz. pkg. yellow cake mix
   with pudding
3.4-oz. pkg. instant lemon
   pudding mix
8-oz. container sour cream
4 eggs, lightly beaten
1/2 c. oil

In a small bowl, combine walnuts, sugar and cinnamon; set aside. In a separate bowl, combine dry cake mix, dry pudding mix, sour cream, eggs and oil. Beat with an electric mixer on medium speed for 2 minutes. Pour into a greased 13"x9" baking pan. Sprinkle half of walnut mixture over batter. Spoon remaining batter evenly over top. Sprinkle with remaining walnut mixture. Bake at 350 degrees for 30 to 35 minutes, until cake tests done. Makes 12 to 16 servings.

**Patty Fosnight
Wildorado, TX**

I always take this tasty coffee cake to brunches. Everyone loves it and asks me for the recipe.

Pumpkin Streusel Coffee Cake

18-1/2 oz. pkg. yellow cake mix
1 c. canned pumpkin
3 eggs, beaten
3 T. oil
1/3 c. water
1 t. pumpkin pie spice
1-1/3 c. brown sugar, packed
   and divided
2 t. cinnamon, divided
1 c. all-purpose flour
1/2 c. butter, softened

In a bowl, combine dry cake mix, pumpkin, eggs, oil, water and pie spice. Pour half the batter into a greased 13"x9" baking pan; set aside remaining batter. Mix together 1/3 cup brown sugar and 3/4 teaspoon cinnamon; sprinkle over batter in pan. Carefully spread remaining batter over cinnamon mixture. Combine flour with remaining brown sugar, remaining cinnamon and butter; mix well. Spread evenly over top. Bake at 325 degrees for 30 to 40 minutes, until a knife tip inserted in the center tests clean. Serves 10 to 12.

Victoria Mitchel
Gettysburg, PA

I adapted my favorite coffee cake recipe to come up with this pumpkin version. It tastes so good with a cup of coffee on a cool fall day.

Whole-Grain Jam Squares

2 c. quick-cooking oats,
  uncooked
1-3/4 c. all-purpose flour
3/4 t. salt
1/2 t. baking soda
1 c. butter, softened
1 c. brown sugar, packed
1/2 c. chopped walnuts
1 t. cinnamon
3/4 to 1 c. strawberry preserves

Combine all ingredients except preserves in a bowl; stir until large crumbs form. Reserve 2 cups oat mixture and set aside. Press remaining mixture into a greased 13"x9" baking pan. Spread preserves over the top; sprinkle with reserved oat mixture. Bake at 400 degrees for 25 to 30 minutes, until golden. Cool; cut into squares. Makes 2 dozen.

Ellen Gibson
Orlando, FL
These look so tempting stacked on a jadite serving plate, and their taste is out of this world.

Yummy Yogurt Muffins

1-1/2 c. all-purpose flour
1 c. sugar
2 t. salt
8-oz. container favorite-flavor
  yogurt
1/2 c. oil
2 eggs, beaten
Optional: cinnamon-sugar

In a bowl, combine all ingredients
except cinnamon-sugar, mixing well.
Fill 12 paper-lined muffin cups
2/3 full with batter. Top each cup
with cinnamon-sugar, if using. Bake
at 350 degrees for 25 to 30 minutes,
until golden. Makes one dozen.

Trisha Donley
Pinedale, WY

These muffins are so fast
and easy to make. With so
many varieties of yogurt,
you could have a different
flavor every time!

INDEX

INDEX

Frosty Orange Juice, page 9

Steak & Egg Breakfast Burrito, page 22

Butterscotch Granola, page 17

Quick Strawberry Cream Danish, page 59

Our Story

Back in 1984, we were next-door neighbors raising our families in the little town of Delaware, Ohio. Two moms with small children, we were looking for a way to do what we loved and stay home with the kids too. We had always shared a love of home cooking and making memories with family & friends and so, after many a conversation over the backyard fence, **Gooseberry Patch** was born.

We put together our first catalog at our kitchen tables, enlisting the help of our loved ones wherever we could. From that very first mailing, we found an immediate connection with many of our customers and it wasn't long before we began receiving letters, photos and recipes from these new friends. In 1992, we put together our very first cookbook, compiled from hundreds of these recipes and, the rest, as they say, is history.

Hard to believe it's been over 25 years since those kitchen-table days! From that original little **Gooseberry Patch** family, we've grown to include an amazing group of creative folks who love cooking, decorating and creating as much as we do. Today, we're best known for our homestyle, family-friendly cookbooks, now recognized as national bestsellers.

One thing's for sure, we couldn't have done it without our friends all across the country. Each year, we're honored to turn thousands of your recipes into our collectible cookbooks. Our hope is that each book captures the stories and heart of all of you who have shared with us. Whether you've been with us since the beginning or are just discovering us, welcome to the **Gooseberry Patch** family!

JoAnn & Vickie

Visit us online:
www.gooseberrypatch.com
1•800•854•6673

U.S. to Canadian Recipe Equivalents

Volume Measurements

1/4 teaspoon	1 mL
1/2 teaspoon	2 mL
1 teaspoon	5 mL
1 tablespoon = 3 teaspoons	15 mL
2 tablespoons = 1 fluid ounce	30 mL
1/4 cup	60 mL
1/3 cup	75 mL
1/2 cup = 4 fluid ounces	125 mL
1 cup = 8 fluid ounces	250 mL
2 cups = 1 pint =16 fluid ounces	500 mL
4 cups = 1 quart	1 L

Weights

1 ounce	30 g
4 ounces	120 g
8 ounces	225 g
16 ounces = 1 pound	450 g

Oven Temperatures

300° F	150° C
325° F	160° C
350° F	180° C
375° F	190° C
400° F	200° C
450° F	230° C

Baking Pan Sizes

Square

8x8x2 inches	2 L = 20x20x5 cm
9x9x2 inches	2.5 L = 23x23x5 cm

Rectangular

13x9x2 inches	3.5 L = 33x23x5 cm

Loaf

9x5x3 inches	2 L = 23x13x7 cm

Round

8x1-1/2 inches	1.2 L = 20x4 cm
9x1-1/2 inches	1.5 L = 23x4 cm

Recipe Abbreviations

t. = teaspoon	ltr. = liter
T. = tablespoon	oz. = ounce
c. = cup	lb. = pound
pt. = pint	doz. = dozen
qt. = quart	pkg. = package
gal. = gallon	env. = envelope

Kitchen Measurements

A pinch = 1/8 tablespoon	1 fluid ounce = 2 tablespoons
3 teaspoons = 1 tablespoon	4 fluid ounces = 1/2 cup
2 tablespoons = 1/8 cup	8 fluid ounces = 1 cup
4 tablespoons = 1/4 cup	16 fluid ounces = 1 pint
8 tablespoons = 1/2 cup	32 fluid ounces = 1 quart
16 tablespoons = 1 cup	16 ounces net weight = 1 pound
2 cups = 1 pint	
4 cups = 1 quart	
4 quarts = 1 gallon	